DIVINE DESSERTS

Consultant Editor:
Valerie Ferguson

southwater

Contents

Introduction

If you are one of the many people who believe that no meal is complete without a dessert, look no further. In *Divine Desserts* you will find delicious sweet dishes ranging from refreshing fruit desserts and creamy mousses to melt-in-the-mouth pastries and sinful hot puddings. The many different ingredients in desserts, such as fruit, nuts, cream, chocolate, coffee, sponge cake, pastry and spices, give each its unique character. Some are deliciously laced with alcohol, which can be replaced with fruit juice for children. Many of the recipes are quick to prepare, making them the ideal end to midweek suppers. Others require a little more forward planning and may be better suited to special occasions. In all cases, easy-to-follow instructions and step-by-step photographs virtually guarantee success.

Some tricky techniques, such as melting chocolate and whisking egg whites, are found in the introduction. It also includes instructions for making professional-looking decorations from flowers and fruit.

Whether you are planning a family supper, a light summery lunch, a romantic dinner or a lavish dinner party, make every occasion special by ending with a divine dessert.

Techniques

Preparing Cake Tins

Instructions vary for preparing cake tins, depending on the mixture and the baking time.

1 To grease a tin: Use butter, margarine or flavourless oil. If using butter or margarine, hold a small piece in kitchen paper (or use your fingers), and rub it all over the base and side of the tin to make a thin, even coating. Brush oil on with a pastry brush.

2 To flour a tin: Put a small scoop of flour in the centre of the greased tin. Tip and rotate the tin so that the flour coats the base and side. Invert and shake out excess flour, tapping to dislodge any pockets of flour.

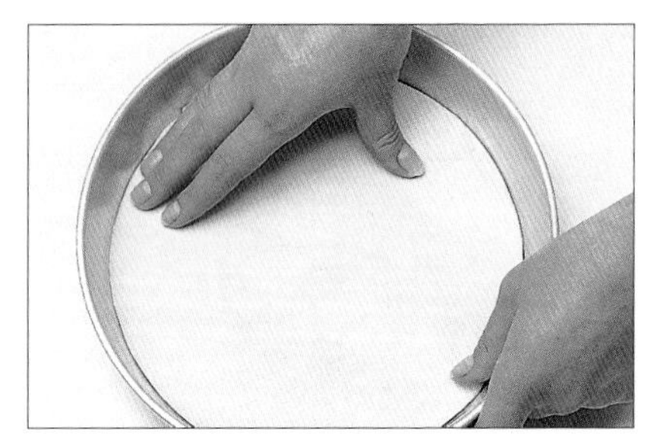

3 To line the base of a tin: Set the tin on a sheet of baking parchment and draw round the base. Cut out this circle, square or rectangle, just inside the drawn line. Press the paper smoothly on to the base of the tin.

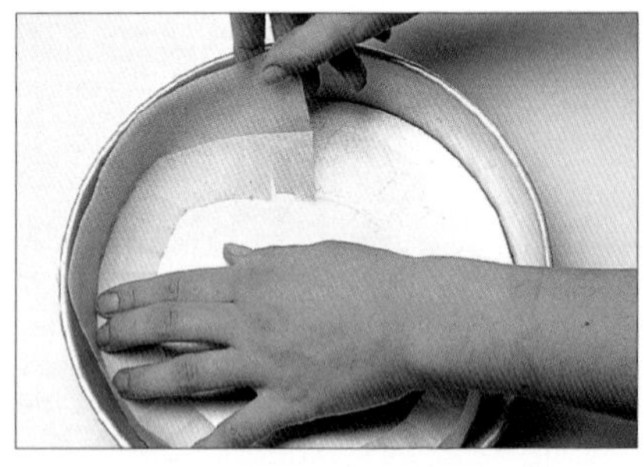

4 To line the sides of a tin: Cut a strip of baking parchment to wrap round the outside of the tin and to overlap itself by 4 cm/1½ in. The strip should be a little wider than the depth of the tin, and should extend above the rim of the tin by 2.5 cm/1 in. Fold the strip lengthways at the 2.5 cm/1 in point and crease. Snip along the fold to the crease. Line the side of the tin, with the snipped part of the strip on the bottom.

Separating Eggs

There are many different ways to separate eggs, but the one that follows is by far the most straightforward.

1 Break the egg shell across the middle on the rim of a bowl.

2 Holding the egg over the bowl, carefully pull the two halves of the shell apart and gently tip the yolk from one half to the other, allowing the white to run down into the bowl. Place the yolk in a separate bowl.

COOK'S TIP: It is not advisable for the very young, the elderly or pregnant women to eat raw eggs.

Whisking Egg Whites

Egg whites can increase in volume by about eight times, making mixtures light and airy. Tap the egg sharply, but not so hard that you break the yolk.

1 Place the egg whites in a completely clean, grease-free mixing bowl. Use one half of the shell to remove any specks of yolk.

2 Using a balloon whisk, whisk the whites until they are firm enough to hold either soft or stiff peaks when you lift the whisk, according to the recipe's requirements. Whisked egg whites should be used immediately.

Melting Chocolate

Chocolate may be melted over hot water or in a microwave oven.

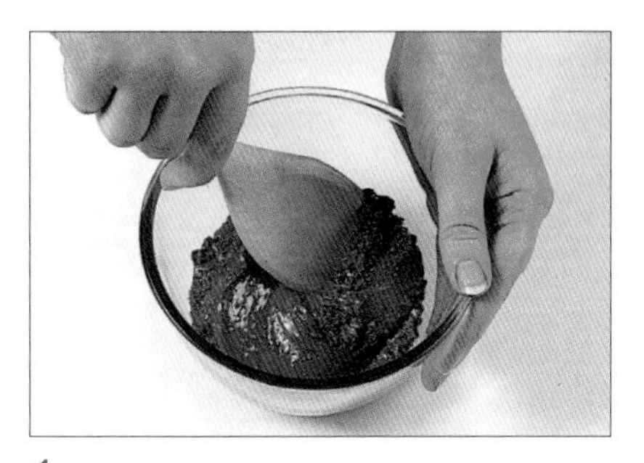

1 To microwave: Break 115 g/4 oz plain chocolate into squares. Place in a heatproof bowl and cook on MEDIUM for 2 minutes. Melt milk and white chocolate in the same way for 2 minutes on LOW. Stir with a wooden spoon.

2 To use hot water: Bring a small pan of water to the boil. Turn off the heat and place the bowl of chocolate over the water. It should not touch the water nor should any drops of water be allowed to fall into it.

3 Leave the chocolate until very soft, then stir it lightly. Melted chocolate can be used in sauces and for decorating cakes and gâteaux.

Crystallized Flowers

These pretty decorations add a delightful touch to any light summery dessert. Put them on the dessert just before you are ready to serve, otherwise they will go soft.

1 Brush flowers and leaves, such as pansies, violas, herb flowers and variegated mint, with raw egg white and sprinkle with caster sugar. Leave to dry for 1–2 hours on a plate or rack out of direct sunlight. Use on the day of making.

Fruit & Flower Decorations

Some of the most eyecatching garnishes and decorations are made from fruit and flowers.

Baby Rose Posy

Choose six perfect small roses and trim the stems to 2.5 cm/1 in. Place five of them in a ring on a gâteau so that the stems meet in the centre. Place the remaining rose on top.

Edible Flowers

Colourful edible flowers, such as nasturtiums, can be used to enliven cold soufflés, mousses and ice cream. Simply scatter several across the plate.

Flower Bouquet

Gather some fresh flowers together in a small bouquet, tie with a ribbon, if you wish, and place on top of a gâteau or mousse for a fragrant decoration.

Orange Flower

Cut two thin slices from an orange, then cut each slice in half. Cut along the inside of the pith on one half to within 3 mm/$\frac{1}{8}$ in of the end. Turn the strip of rind in to form a loop that rests against the half slice. Repeat with the remaining half slices. Place them in a ring with the loops on the outside. This looks stunning on chocolate desserts.

Pear Fan

Peel a pear, leaving the stem intact. Poach in a light syrup until tender. Cut in half lengthways and core. Place cut-side down and cut about eight thin slices, leaving them intact at the top. Press down gently to fan the slices apart. Use these fans for chocolate and fruit desserts.

Strawberry Fan

Cut a strawberry into thin slices from the pointed end almost to the top. Leave the hull and calyx in place and gently fan out the slices. Use to decorate fruit desserts and mousses.

Fresh Fig, Apple & Date Salad

Sweet Mediterranean figs and dates combine especially well with crisp dessert apples. A hint of almond serves to unite the flavours.

Serves 4

INGREDIENTS
6 large apples
juice of ½ lemon
175 g/6 oz fresh dates
25 g/1 oz white marzipan
5 ml/1 tsp orange flower water
60 ml/4 tbsp natural yogurt
4 green or purple figs
4 almonds, toasted

1 Core the apples. Slice thinly, then cut the slices into fine matchsticks. Moisten with lemon juice to stop them from turning brown.

2 Carefully remove the stones from the fresh dates and cut the flesh into fine strips, then combine with the apple matchsticks.

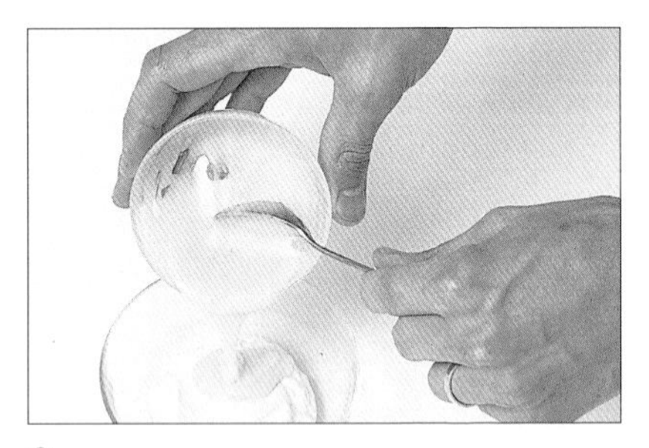

3 Soften the marzipan with the orange flower water in a small bowl and combine with the yogurt. Mix well.

4 Pile the apples and dates in the centre of four plates. Remove the stem from each of the figs and divide the fruit into quarters, without cutting right through the base. Squeeze the base with the thumb and forefinger of each hand to open up the fruit.

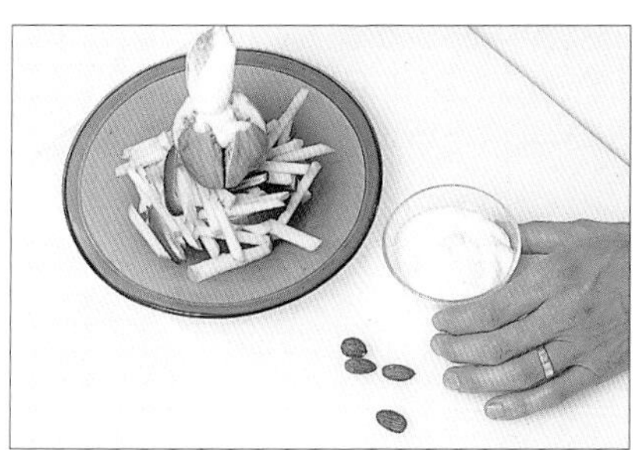

5 Place an opened fig in the centre of the apple and date salad and spoon in the yogurt, marzipan and orange flower filling. Decorate the filling with a whole toasted almond.

Clementines with Star Anise & Cinnamon

This fresh dessert, delicately flavoured with mulling spices, makes the perfect ending for a festive meal.

Serves 6

INGREDIENTS
350 ml/12 fl oz/1½ cups sweet dessert wine
75 g/3 oz/⅓ cup caster sugar
6 star anise
1 cinnamon stick
1 vanilla pod
1 strip of thinly pared lime rind
30 ml/2 tbsp Cointreau
12 clementines

1 Put the wine, sugar, star anise and cinnamon in a saucepan. Split the vanilla pod and add it to the pan with the lime rind.

2 Bring to the boil, lower the heat and simmer for 10 minutes. Allow to cool, then stir in the Cointreau.

3 Peel the clementines, removing all the pith and white membranes. Cut some of the clementines in half and arrange them all in a glass dish. Pour over the spiced wine and chill overnight before serving.

VARIATION: Tangerines or oranges can be used instead of clementines if you prefer.

Grilled Spiced Fruit Kebabs

These colourful, lightly spiced kebabs are a tempting treat and very quick and easy to prepare and cook.

Serves 4–6

INGREDIENTS
4–5 kinds of firm ripe fruit, such as pineapple and mango cubes, strawberry and pear slices, grapes and tangerine segments
25 g/1 oz/2 tbsp unsalted butter, melted
grated rind and juice of 1 orange
sugar to taste
pinch of ground cinnamon or nutmeg
yogurt, soured cream or crème fraîche, to serve

1 Preheat the grill and line a baking sheet with foil. If using wooden skewers, soak them in cold water.

2 Thread the fruit on 4–6 skewers. Arrange the skewers on the prepared baking sheet, spoon over the melted butter, orange rind and juice and sprinkle with sugar to taste, together with a pinch of cinnamon or nutmeg.

3 Grill the kebabs for 2–3 minutes, turning once, until the sugar is just beginning to caramelize. Serve with yogurt, soured cream or crème fraîche.

Pears in Chocolate Fudge Blankets

Warm poached pears swathed in a rich chocolate fudge sauce – who could resist such a sensual pleasure?

Serves 6

INGREDIENTS
6 ripe eating pears
30 ml/2 tbsp lemon juice
75 g/3 oz/⅓ cup caster sugar
300 ml/½ pint/1¼ cups water
1 cinnamon stick

FOR THE SAUCE
200 ml/7 fl oz/scant 1 cup double cream
150 g/5 oz/scant 1 cup light muscovado sugar
25 g/1 oz/2 tbsp unsalted butter
60 ml/4 tbsp golden syrup
120 ml/4 fl oz/½ cup milk
200 g/7 oz plain dark chocolate, broken into squares

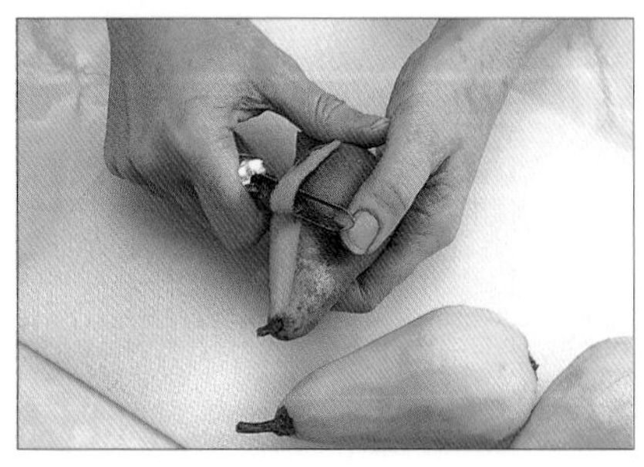

1 Peel the pears thinly, leaving the stalks on. Scoop out the cores from the base. Brush the cut surfaces with lemon juice to prevent browning.

2 Place the sugar and water in a large saucepan. Heat gently until the sugar dissolves. Add the pears and cinnamon stick with any remaining lemon juice, and, if necessary, a little more water, so that the pears are almost covered.

3 Bring to the boil, then lower the heat, cover and simmer gently for 15–20 minutes, or until the pears are just tender.

4 Meanwhile, make the sauce. Place the cream, sugar, butter, golden syrup and milk in a heavy-based saucepan. Heat gently until the sugar has dissolved and the butter and syrup have melted, then bring to the boil. Boil, stirring constantly, for about 5 minutes or until thick and smooth.

5 Remove the pan from the heat and stir in the dark chocolate, a few squares at a time, until it has melted.

6 Using a slotted spoon, transfer the poached pears to a dish. Keep hot. Boil the syrup rapidly to reduce to about 45–60 ml/3–4 tbsp. Remove the cinnamon stick and stir the syrup into the chocolate sauce. Serve the pears in individual bowls, with the hot chocolate sauce spooned over.

Fruit Gratin

This out-of-the-ordinary gratin is strictly for grown-ups.

Serves 4

INGREDIENTS
2 tamarillos
½ sweet pineapple
1 ripe mango, peeled
175 g/6 oz/1½ cups blackberries
120 ml/4 fl oz/½ cup sparkling white wine
115 g/4 oz/½ cup caster sugar
6 egg yolks

1 Cut the tamarillos in half lengthways and then into thick slices. Cut the rind and core from the pineapple and remove the eyes. Cut the flesh into chunks. Cut the mango in half and slice the flesh from the stone.

2 Divide all the fruit among four gratin dishes set on a baking sheet. Heat the wine and sugar in a saucepan until the sugar has dissolved. Bring to the boil and cook for 5 minutes.

3 Put the egg yolks in a heatproof bowl set over a pan of simmering water and whisk until pale. Slowly pour on the hot sugar syrup, whisking, until the mixture thickens. Preheat the grill.

4 Spoon the mixture over the fruit. Place the baking sheet under the grill until the topping is golden. Serve hot.

Fruit Gratin (top); Hot Pineapple

Hot Pineapple

This dessert is delicious served with the papaya sauce.

Serves 6

INGREDIENTS
1 sweet pineapple
melted butter, for greasing and brushing
2 pieces drained stem ginger in syrup, cut into fine matchsticks, plus 30 ml/2 tbsp of the syrup from the jar
30 ml/2 tbsp demerara sugar
pinch of ground cinnamon
fresh mint sprigs, to decorate

FOR THE SAUCE
1 ripe papaya, peeled and seeded
175 ml/6 fl oz/¾ cup apple juice

1 Peel the pineapple and remove the eyes. Cut it crossways into six slices. Line a baking sheet with foil, rolling up the sides to make a rim, and grease with melted butter. Preheat the grill.

2 Arrange the pineapple on the foil. Brush with butter, then top with the ginger, sugar and cinnamon. Drizzle with syrup. Grill for 5–7 minutes.

3 Meanwhile, make the sauce. Cut a few slices from the papaya and set aside, then process the rest with the apple juice in a blender or food processor. Press through a sieve, then stir in any juices from cooking the pineapple. Serve the pineapple with sauce, decorated with papaya and mint.

Stuffed Peaches with Amaretto

Together amaretti biscuits and amaretto liqueur have an intense almond flavour, and they make a natural partner for peaches.

Serves 4

INGREDIENTS
4 ripe but firm peaches
50 g/2 oz amaretti biscuits
25 g/1 oz/2 tbsp butter, softened, plus extra, for greasing
25 g/1 oz/2 tbsp caster sugar
1 egg yolk
60 ml/4 tbsp amaretto liqueur
250 ml/8 fl oz/1 cup dry white wine
sprigs of mint, to decorate
ice cream or pouring cream, to serve

1 Preheat the oven to 180°C/350°F/ Gas 4. Following the natural indentation line on each peach, cut in half down to the central stone, then twist the halves in opposite directions to separate them.

2 Remove the peach stones, then cut away a little of the central flesh to make a larger hole for the stuffing. Chop this flesh finely and set aside.

COOK'S TIP: You might find it easier to crush the amaretti biscuits in a knotted plastic bag instead of in a bowl.

3 Put the amaretti biscuits in a bowl and crush them finely with the end of a rolling pin.

4 Cream the butter and sugar together in a separate bowl until smooth. Stir in the reserved chopped peach flesh, the egg yolk and half the amaretto liqueur with the prepared amaretti crumbs.

5 Lightly butter an ovenproof dish that is just large enough to hold the peach halves in a single layer.

VARIATION: This dish also looks most attractive decorated with tiny sprigs of fresh basil, if available.

6 Spoon the stuffing into the peaches, then stand them in the dish. Mix the remaining liqueur with the wine, pour over the peaches and bake them for 25 minutes, or until they feel tender when tested with a skewer. Decorate with mint sprigs and serve hot, with ice cream or cream, if liked.

Mango Ice Cream

Home-made ice cream is utterly delicious and surprisingly easy to make. Serve this delicately flavoured dessert at the end of a dinner party.

Serves 4–6

INGREDIENTS
2 x 425 g/15 oz cans sliced mango, drained
50 g/2 oz/¼ cup caster sugar
30 ml/2 tbsp lime juice
15 ml/1 tbsp powdered gelatine
350 ml/12 fl oz/1½ cups double cream, lightly whipped
fresh mint sprigs, to decorate

1 Reserve four slices of mango for decoration and chop the remainder. Place the mangoes in a bowl with the sugar and lime juice. Stir well.

COOK'S TIP: Although fresh mango can be used instead, the canned variety makes this dish especially easy to prepare and tastes just as good.

2 Put 45 ml/3 tbsp hot water in a small heatproof bowl and sprinkle over the gelatine. Place over a pan of gently simmering water and stir until dissolved. Pour on to the mangoes and mix well.

3 Add the lightly whipped cream and fold into the mango mixture. Pour the mixture into a plastic freezer container and freeze until half frozen.

4 Place in a food processor or blender and process until smooth. Spoon back into the container and re-freeze.

5 Remove the ice cream from the freezer 10 minutes before serving and place in the fridge. Serve in scoops, decorated with pieces of the reserved sliced mango and fresh mint.

VARIATION: You might like to try using other canned fruit, such as pineapple, to make equally simple ice cream.

Frosted Raspberry & Coffee Terrine

A white chocolate and raspberry layer and a contrasting smooth coffee layer make this attractive-looking dessert doubly delicious.

Serves 6–8

INGREDIENTS
30 ml/2 tbsp flavoured ground coffee, e.g. mocha or orange
250 ml/8 fl oz/1 cup milk
4 eggs, separated
50 g/2 oz/¼ cup caster sugar
30 ml/2 tbsp cornflour
150 ml/¼ pint/⅔ cup double cream
150 g/5 oz white chocolate, roughly chopped
115 g/4 oz/⅔ cup raspberries
shavings of white chocolate and cocoa powder, to decorate

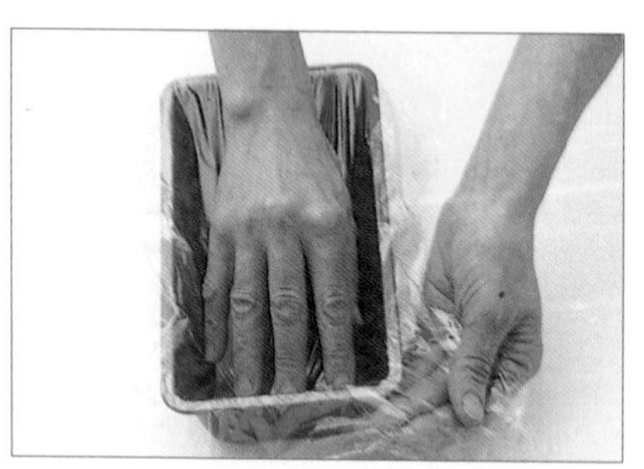

1 Line a 1.5 litre/2½ pint/6¼ cup loaf tin with clear film and put in the freezer to chill. Put the ground coffee in a jug. Heat 100 ml/3½ fl oz/scant ½ cup of the milk to near-boiling point and pour over the coffee. Leave to infuse.

2 Blend the egg yolks, sugar and cornflour together in a saucepan and whisk in the remaining milk and the cream. Bring to the boil, stirring constantly, until thickened.

3 Divide the hot mixture between two bowls and add the white chocolate to one, stirring until melted. Strain the coffee through a fine nylon sieve into the other bowl and mix well. Leave until cool, stirring occasionally.

4 Whisk two of the egg whites until stiff. Fold into the coffee custard. Spoon into the tin and freeze for 30 minutes. Whisk the remaining whites and fold into the chocolate mixture with the raspberries.

5 Spoon the chocolate mixture into the tin and level before freezing for 4 hours. Turn the terrine out on to a flat serving plate and peel off the clear film. Cover with chocolate shavings and dust with cocoa powder.

COOK'S TIP: After decorating, allow the terrine to soften in the fridge for 20 minutes before slicing.

Chilled Chocolate & Espresso Mousse

Heady, aromatic espresso coffee adds a distinctive flavour to this smooth, rich mousse. Serve it in stylish chocolate cups for a special occasion.

Serves 4

INGREDIENTS
small orange, for moulding cups
225 g/8 oz plain chocolate
45 ml/3 tbsp brewed espresso
25 g/1 oz/2 tbsp unsalted butter
4 eggs, separated
sprigs of fresh mint,
to decorate (optional)
mascarpone or clotted cream,
to serve (optional)

FOR THE CHOCOLATE CUPS
225 g/8 oz plain chocolate

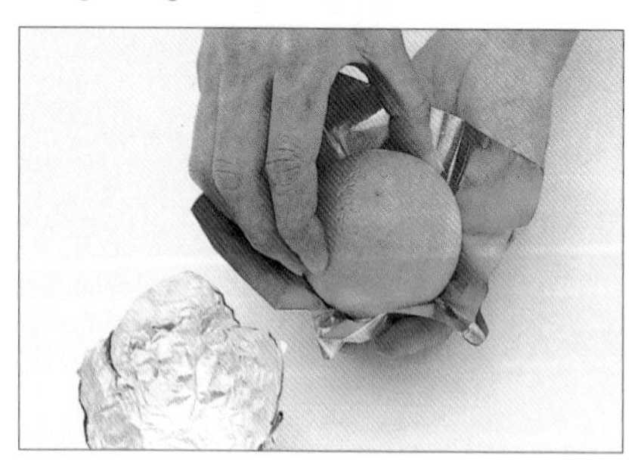

1 For each chocolate cup, cut a double thickness 15 cm/6 in square of foil. Mould it around a small orange, leaving the edges and corners loose to make a cup shape. Remove the orange and press the bottom of the foil case gently on a surface to make a flat base. Repeat to make four foil cups.

2 Break the plain chocolate for the cups into small pieces and place in a heatproof bowl set over a pan of very hot water. Stir occasionally until the chocolate has melted.

3 Spoon the melted chocolate into the foil cups, spreading it up the sides of the cups with the back of a spoon to give a ragged edge. Refrigerate for 30 minutes, or until the chocolate has set hard. Gently peel away the foil cases, starting at the top edge.

4 To make the chocolate mousse, put the chocolate and brewed espresso into a bowl set over a pan of hot water and melt. When the mixture is smooth and liquid, add the butter, a little at a time. Remove the pan from the heat, then stir in the egg yolks.

5 Whisk the egg whites in a bowl until stiff, but not dry, then fold them into the chocolate mixture. Pour into a bowl and refrigerate for at least 3 hours.

6 To serve, scoop the chilled mousse into the chocolate cups. Add a scoop of mascarpone or clotted cream and decorate with a sprig of fresh mint, if you wish.

Frozen Raspberry Mousse

This dessert is like a frozen soufflé. Freeze it in a ring mould, then fill the centre with raspberries flavoured with orange juice or liqueur.

Serves 6

INGREDIENTS
350 g/12 oz/2 cups raspberries, plus
150 g/5 oz/scant 1 cup extra, for serving
45 ml/3 tbsp icing sugar
2 egg whites
1.5 ml/¼ tsp cream of tartar
90 g/3½ oz/½ cup granulated sugar
25 ml/1½ tbsp lemon juice
250 ml/8 fl oz/1 cup whipping cream
15 ml/1 tbsp *framboise* or orange juice
mint leaves, to decorate

1 Process the raspberries in a food processor until smooth, then press through a sieve or work through the fine blade of a food mill. Pour a third of the purée into a small bowl, stir in the icing sugar, cover and chill. Reserve the remaining purée.

2 Half-fill a medium saucepan with hot water and set over a low heat (do not allow it to boil). Combine the egg whites, cream of tartar, sugar and lemon juice in a heatproof bowl which just fits into the pan without touching the water.

3 Using an electric mixer, beat at medium speed until the beaters leave tracks on the base of the bowl, then beat at high speed for 7 minutes, until the mixture is thick and forms peaks.

4 Remove the bowl from the pan and beat the mixture for a further 2–3 minutes, until cool. Fold in the reserved raspberry purée.

5 Whip the cream until it forms soft peaks and fold into the raspberry mixture with the liqueur or orange juice. Spoon into a 1.5 litre/2½ pint/6¼ cup ring mould, cover and freeze for at least 4 hours.

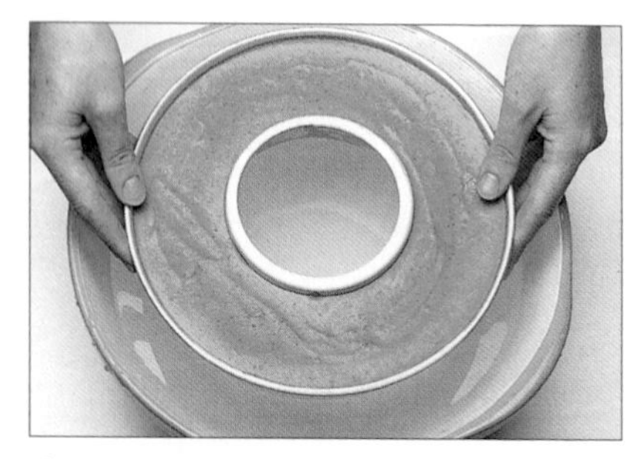

6 To unmould, dip the mould in warm water and invert on to a serving plate. Fill the centre of the mousse with raspberries, decorate with mint and serve with the chilled purée.

Lemon Soufflé with Caramelized Almond Topping

This refreshing soufflé with a delectable topping is light and luscious.

Serves 6

INGREDIENTS
oil, for greasing
grated rind and juice of 3 large lemons
5 large eggs, separated
115 g/4 oz/½ cup caster sugar
25 ml/1½ tbsp powdered gelatine
450 ml/¾ pint/scant 2 cups double cream

FOR THE DECORATION
75 g/3 oz/¾ cup flaked almonds
75 g/3 oz/¾ cup icing sugar
3 physalis (Cape gooseberries)

1 Cut a strip of non-stick baking parchment long enough to fit around a 900 ml/1½ pint/3¾ cup soufflé dish and wide enough to extend 7.5 cm/ 3 in above the rim. Fit around the dish, tape, then tie it around the top of the dish with string. Brush the inside of the paper lightly with oil.

2 Put the lemon rind and egg yolks in a bowl. Add 75 g/3 oz/⅓ cup of the caster sugar and whisk until light and creamy. Place the lemon juice in a heatproof bowl and sprinkle over the gelatine. Set aside for 5 minutes, then place the bowl in a pan of simmering water. Heat, stirring, until the gelatine has dissolved. Cool slightly, then stir into the egg yolk mixture.

3 In a separate bowl, lightly whip the cream to soft peaks. Fold into the egg yolk mixture and set aside.

4 Whisk the egg whites until stiff peaks form. Gradually whisk in the remaining sugar until the mixture is stiff and glossy. Fold the whites into the yolk mixture. Pour into the prepared dish, smooth the surface and chill for 4–5 hours, or until set.

5 Make the decoration. Brush a baking sheet with oil. Preheat the grill. Scatter the almonds over the sheet and sift the icing sugar over. Grill until the nuts are golden and the sugar has caramelized. Cool, then remove from the tray with a palette knife and break it into pieces.

6 When the soufflé has set, carefully peel off the paper. Pile the caramelized almonds on top of the soufflé and decorate with the physalis.

Rose-petal Sorbet

This sorbet makes a wonderful end to a summer meal with its fabulous flavour of roses. Remember to use the most scented variety of rose that you can find in the garden.

Serves 4–6

INGREDIENTS
115 g/4 oz/½ cup caster sugar
300 ml/½ pint/1¼ cups boiling water
petals of 3 large, scented red or deep-pink roses, white ends of petals removed
juice of 2 lemons
300 ml/½ pint/1¼ cups rosé wine
whole crystallized roses or rose petals, to serve

1 Place the sugar in a bowl and add the boiling water. Stir until the sugar has completely dissolved. Add the rose petals and leave to cool completely.

2 Process the mixture in a food processor, then strain. Add the lemon juice and wine and pour into a freezer container. Freeze for several hours, until the mixture has frozen around the edges.

3 Turn the sorbet into a mixing bowl and whisk until smooth. Re-freeze until frozen around the edges. Repeat the whisking and freezing process once or twice more, until the sorbet is pale and smooth. Freeze until firm.

4 Serve the sorbet in individual glass bowls, decorated with crystallized roses or rose petals.

COOK'S TIP: This sorbet can also be made in an ice cream maker. Churn until firm with a good texture. If the sorbet is too hard, transfer it to the fridge for about 30 minutes before serving.

Fresh Berry Pavlova

Pavlova is the simplest of desserts, but it can also be the most stunning. Fill with a mix of berry fruits if you like – raspberries and blueberries make a marvellous combination.

Serves 6–8

INGREDIENTS
4 egg whites, at room temperature
225 g/8 oz/1 cup caster sugar
5 ml/1 tsp cornflour
5 ml/1 tsp cider vinegar
2.5 ml/½ tsp vanilla essence
300 ml/½ pint/1¼ cups double cream
150 ml/¼ pint/⅔ cup crème fraîche
175 g/6 oz/1 cup raspberries
175 g/6 oz/1½ cups blueberries
fresh mint sprigs, to decorate
icing sugar, for dusting

1 Preheat the oven to 140°C/275°F/Gas 1. Line a baking sheet with non-stick baking parchment.

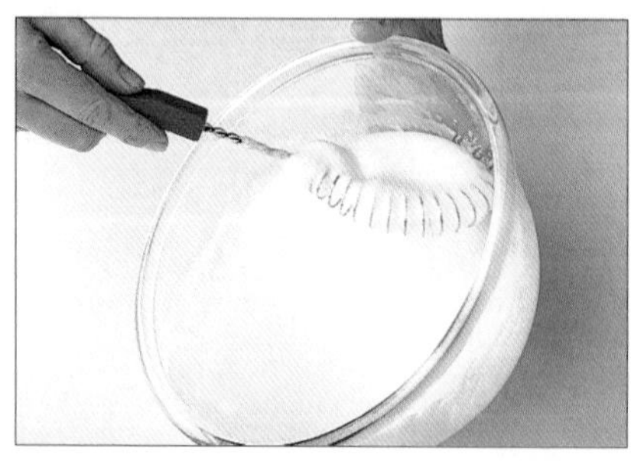

2 Whisk the egg whites until they form stiff peaks. Gradually whisk in the sugar to make a stiff, glossy meringue. Sift the cornflour over and fold it in with the vinegar and vanilla.

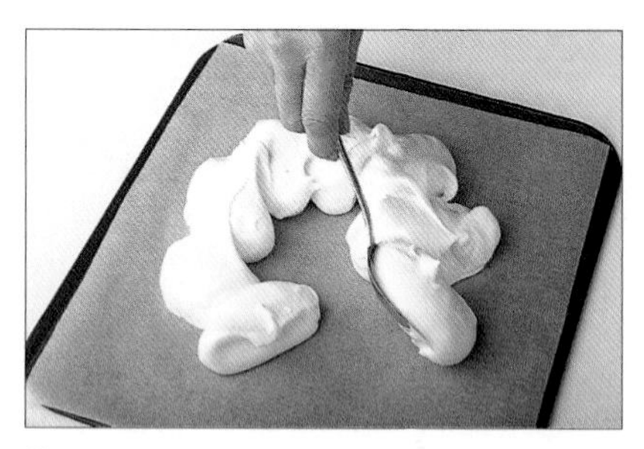

3 Spoon the meringue mixture on to the paper-lined sheet, using the circle drawn on the paper as a guide (see Cook's Tip). Spread into a round, swirling the top, and bake for 1¼ hours or until the meringue is crisp and very lightly golden.

4 Switch off the oven, keeping the door closed, and allow the meringue to cool gradually for 1–2 hours.

5 Carefully peel the paper from underneath the meringue and transfer it to a serving plate.

COOK'S TIP: To begin, invert a 23 cm/9 in plate on the baking parchment and draw round it with a pencil. Turn the paper over and use the circle as a guide for the shape of the meringue.

6 Whip the double cream in a large mixing bowl until it forms soft peaks. Fold in the crème fraîche, then spoon the mixture into the centre of the meringue case.

7 Top with the raspberries and blueberries and decorate with the mint sprigs. Sift icing sugar over the top and serve at once.

Peach & Redcurrant Tartlets

Tart redcurrants and sweet peaches make a winning combination in these simple, but very appealing little tartlets.

Serves 4

INGREDIENTS
25 g/1 oz/2 tbsp butter, melted
16 x 15 cm/6 in squares of filo pastry, thawed if frozen
icing sugar, for dusting
redcurrant sprigs, to decorate

FOR THE FILLING
150 ml/¼ pint/⅔ cup double cream
125 g/4¼ oz carton peach and mango fromage frais
a few drops of vanilla essence
15 ml/1 tbsp icing sugar, sifted

FOR THE TOPPING
50 g/2 oz/½ cup redcurrants
2 peaches

1 Preheat the oven to 190°C/375°F/Gas 5. Use a little of the butter to grease four large bun tins or individual tartlet tins. Brush the pastry squares with butter, stack in fours, then place in the tins to make four pastry cases.

2 Bake for 12–15 minutes until golden. Cool the cases on a wire rack.

3 Whip the cream to form soft peaks, then fold in the peach and mango fromage frais, vanilla essence and icing sugar. Divide among the cases.

4 Strip some of the redcurrants from their stalks by pulling the stalks through the tines of a fork.

5 Slice the peaches and fan them out on top of the filling, interspersing with a few redcurrants. Decorate the tartlets with the redcurrant sprigs and dust with icing sugar before serving.

Kiwi Fruit Roulade

This sophisticated dessert just melts in the mouth and would make the perfect end to a formal dinner party.

Serves 6

INGREDIENTS
12–16 young geranium leaves
5 eggs, separated
275 g/10 oz/2¼ cups caster sugar
30 ml/2 tbsp icing sugar, plus extra for dusting
a few drops of rose water
300 ml/½ pint/1¼ cups double cream
2 kiwi fruit
10–15 fresh or crystallized geranium petals

1 Preheat the oven to 180°C/350°F/Gas 4. Line a 20 x 28 cm/8 x 11 in baking tray with greaseproof paper and lay the geranium leaves all over it.

2 Beat together the egg yolks and caster sugar until the mixture is light and fluffy.

3 In a separate bowl, whisk the egg whites until they are stiff and then fold into the egg yolk and sugar mixture until it is smooth.

4 Pour the mixture on top of the geranium leaves on the baking tray and bake for about 10 minutes, until just set. Remove from the oven and leave to cool.

5 Turn the roulade out on to a clean piece of greaseproof paper dusted with 30 ml/2 tbsp icing sugar. Carefully remove the geranium leaves.

6 Add a few drops of rose water to the cream and then whip until soft peaks form.

7 Spread the whipped cream over the roulade. Peel and thinly slice the kiwi fruit and distribute the slices over the surface of the cream.

8 Roll up the roulade, holding the short edges. Dust with icing sugar and arrange the petals on top.

Raspberry Shortcake

Rose water cream and fresh raspberries form the filling for this delectable dessert, which is actually quite easy to make.

Serves 6

INGREDIENTS
115 g/4 oz/½ cup unsalted butter, softened
50 g/2 oz/¼ cup caster sugar
½ vanilla pod, split, seeds reserved
115 g/4 oz/1 cup plain flour, plus extra for dusting
50 g/2 oz/⅓ cup semolina
icing sugar, for dusting

FOR THE FILLING
300 ml/½ pint/1¼ cups double cream
15 ml/1 tbsp icing sugar
2.5 ml/½ tsp rose water
450 g/1 lb/2⅔ cups raspberries

FOR THE DECORATION
12 miniature roses, unsprayed
1 egg white, beaten
caster sugar, for dusting
6 mint sprigs

1 Cream the butter, caster sugar and vanilla seeds until pale and fluffy. Sift the flour and semolina together, then gradually work into the creamed mixture to make a biscuit dough.

2 Knead the dough on a lightly floured surface until smooth. Roll out quite thinly and prick all over with a fork. Using a 7.5 cm/3 in fluted cutter, cut out 12 rounds. Place on a baking sheet and chill for 30 minutes.

3 Meanwhile, make the filling. Whisk the cream with the icing sugar until soft peaks form. Fold in the rose water and chill until required.

4 Preheat the oven to 180°C/350°F/Gas 4. To make the decoration, paint the roses and leaves with the egg white. Dust with caster sugar, then dry on a wire rack.

5 Bake the shortcakes for 15 minutes, or until lightly golden. Lift them off the baking sheet with a metal fish slice and cool on a wire rack.

6 To assemble the shortcakes, spoon the rose water cream on to half the biscuits. Add a layer of raspberries, then top with a second shortcake. Dust with icing sugar. Decorate with the frosted roses and mint sprigs.

COOK'S TIP: For best results, serve the shortcakes as soon as possible after assembling them. Otherwise, they are likely to turn soggy from the berries' liquid.

Meringue Gâteau with Chocolate Mascarpone

This superb gâteau makes the perfect centrepiece for a celebration buffet table, and most of the preparation can be done in advance.

Serves 10

INGREDIENTS
4 egg whites
pinch of salt
175 g/6 oz/¾ cup caster sugar
5 ml/1 tsp ground cinnamon
75 g/3 oz plain dark chocolate, grated
icing sugar and rose petals, to decorate

FOR THE FILLING
115 g/4 oz plain chocolate, broken into squares
5 ml/1 tsp vanilla essence or rose water
115 g/4 oz/½ cup Mascarpone

1 Preheat the oven to 150°C/300°F/Gas 2. Line two large baking sheets with non-stick baking parchment. Whisk the egg whites with the salt in a greasefree bowl to form stiff peaks.

2 Gradually whisk in half the sugar, then add the rest and whisk until the meringue is very stiff and glossy. Add the cinnamon and chocolate and whisk lightly to mix.

COOK'S TIP: The meringues can be made up to a week in advance and stored in an airtight container in a cool, dry place.

3 Draw a 20 cm/8 in circle on the lining paper on one of the baking sheets, replace it upside-down and spread the marked circle evenly with about half the meringue. Spoon the remaining meringue into 28–30 small neat heaps on both baking sheets. Bake for 1–1½ hours, or until crisp.

4 Make the filling. Melt the chocolate in a heatproof bowl over a pan of gently simmering water. Cool slightly, then add the vanilla essence or rose water and Mascarpone. Cool the mixture until it holds its shape.

5 Spoon the chocolate mixture into a large piping bag and sandwich the meringues together in pairs, reserving a small amount of filling for the gâteau.

6 Arrange the filled meringues on top of the meringue circle on a serving platter, piling them up in a pyramid and securing them with a few well-placed dabs of the reserved filling. Dust the gâteau with icing sugar, sprinkle with the rose petals and serve.

Coffee Cream Profiteroles

Crisp-textured coffee choux pastry puffs are filled with cream and drizzled with a white chocolate sauce.

Serves 6

INGREDIENTS
65 g/2½ oz/9 tbsp plain white flour
pinch of salt
50 g/2 oz/¼ cup butter
150 ml/¼ pint/⅔ cup brewed coffee
2 eggs, lightly beaten
cocoa powder, for dusting

FOR THE WHITE CHOCOLATE SAUCE
50 g/2 oz/¼ cup granulated sugar
100 ml/3½ fl oz/scant ½ cup water
150 g/5 oz white dessert chocolate, broken into pieces
25 g/1 oz/2 tbsp unsalted butter
45 ml/3 tbsp double cream
30 ml/2 tbsp coffee liqueur, such as Tía Maria, Kahlúa or Toussaint

TO ASSEMBLE
250 ml/8 fl oz/1 cup double cream

1 Preheat the oven to 220°C/425°F/Gas 7. Sift the flour and salt on to a piece of greaseproof paper. Cut the butter into pieces and put in a pan with the coffee.

2 Bring to a rolling boil, then remove the pan from the heat and tip in all the flour. Beat until the mixture leaves the sides of the pan. Leave to cool for 2 minutes.

3 Gradually add the eggs, beating well between each addition. Spoon the mixture into a piping bag fitted with a 1 cm/½ in plain nozzle.

4 Pipe about 24 small buns on to a dampened baking sheet. Bake for 20 minutes, until the buns are well risen and crisp.

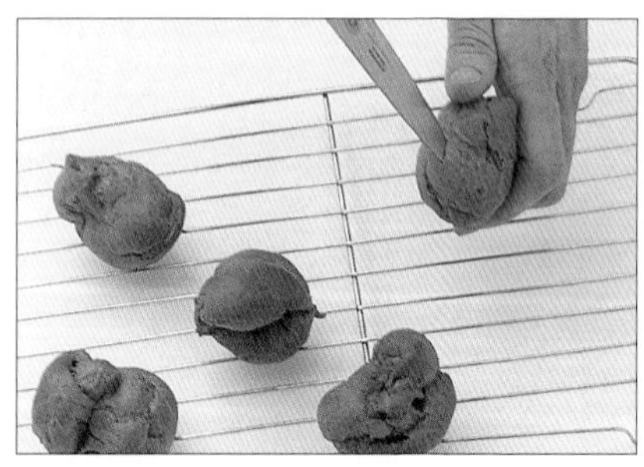

5 Remove the buns from the oven and pierce the side of each with a sharp knife to let out the steam. Cool on a wire rack.

6 To make the sauce, put the sugar and water in a heavy-based pan and heat gently until dissolved. Bring to the boil and simmer for 3 minutes. Remove from the heat. Add the chocolate and butter, stirring until smooth. Stir in the cream and liqueur.

7 To assemble, whip the cream until soft peaks form. Using a piping bag, fill the choux buns through the slits in the sides. Arrange on plates and pour a little of the sauce over, either warm or at room temperature. Dust with cocoa and serve with the remaining sauce.

Chocolate Soufflés

These soufflés are easy to make and can be prepared in advance – the filled dishes can wait for up to one hour before baking.

Serves 6

INGREDIENTS
150 g/5 oz/⅔ cup unsalted butter, cut in small pieces, plus extra for greasing
175 g/6 oz plain chocolate, chopped
4 large eggs, separated
30 ml/2 tbsp orange liqueur (optional)
45 ml/3 tbsp caster sugar, plus extra for sprinkling
1.5 ml/¼ tsp cream of tartar
icing sugar, for dusting
redcurrants and white chocolate curls, to garnish

FOR THE WHITE CHOCOLATE SAUCE
75 g/3 oz white chocolate, chopped
90 ml/6 tbsp whipping cream
15–30 ml/1–2 tbsp orange liqueur
finely grated rind of ½ orange

1 Generously butter six 150 ml/¼ pint/⅔ cup ramekins. Sprinkle each with a little caster sugar and tap out any excess. Place the ramekins on a baking sheet.

2 In a heavy saucepan over a very low heat, melt the chocolate and butter, stirring until smooth.

VARIATION: Instead of orange liqueur, try using brandy or coffee liqueur in the soufflés and sauce.

3 Cool slightly, then beat in the egg yolks and orange liqueur, if using. Set aside, stirring occasionally.

4 Preheat the oven to 220°C/425°F/Gas 7. In a greasefree bowl, whisk the egg whites slowly until frothy. Add the cream of tartar, increase the speed and whisk to soft peaks. Sprinkle over the sugar, 15 ml/1 tbsp at a time, whisking until stiff and glossy.

5 Stir a third of the whites into the cooled chocolate mixture, then pour over the remaining whites. Gently fold the sauce into the whites. Spoon into the prepared dishes.

6 For the sauce, put the chocolate and cream in a pan over a low heat and stir constantly until melted and smooth. Off the heat, stir in the liqueur and orange rind. Keep warm.

7 Bake the soufflés for 10–12 minutes, until risen and set, but still slightly wobbly. Dust with icing sugar and serve with the sauce, garnished with redcurrants and chocolate curls.

Apricot Parcels

These little filo parcels contain a special apricot and mincemeat filling – a good way to use up any mincemeat and marzipan that have been in your cupboard since Christmas!

Makes 8

INGREDIENTS
350 g/12 oz filo pastry, thawed if frozen
50 g/2 oz/¼ cup butter, melted
60 ml/4 tbsp luxury mincemeat
12 ratafias, crushed
30 ml/2 tbsp grated marzipan
8 apricots, halved and stoned
icing sugar, for dusting

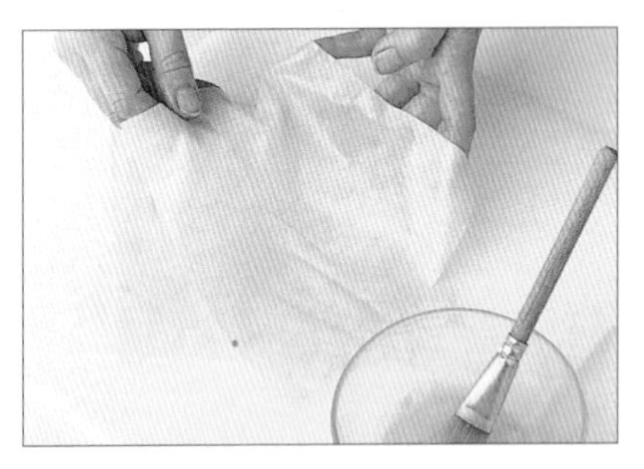

1 Preheat the oven to 200°C/400°F/ Gas 6. Cut the filo pastry into 32 x 18 cm/7 in squares. Brush four of the squares with a little melted butter and stack them, giving each layer a quarter turn so that the stack acquires a star shape. Repeat to make eight stars.

2 Mix together the mincemeat, crushed ratafias and marzipan and spoon a little of the mixture into the hollow in each of the apricots. Top with another apricot half.

3 Place a filled apricot in the centre of each pastry star. Bring the corners of the pastry together and squeeze to make a gathered purse.

4 Place the purses on a baking sheet and brush each with a little melted butter. Bake for 15–20 minutes, or until the pastry is golden and crisp. Lightly dust with icing sugar to serve.

COOK'S TIP: Filo pastry dries out quickly, so keep any squares not currently being used covered under a clean, damp dish towel. Also, try to work as quickly as possible. If the filo should turn dry and brittle, simply brush it with a little melted butter to moisten.

Apple Crêpes with Butterscotch Sauce

These wonderful dessert crêpes are flavoured with sweet cider, filled with caramelized apples and drizzled with a rich, smooth butterscotch sauce.

Serves 4

INGREDIENTS
115 g/4 oz/1 cup plain flour
pinch of salt
2 eggs
175 ml/6 fl oz/¾ cup creamy milk
120 ml/4 fl oz/½ cup sweet cider
butter, for frying

FOR THE FILLING AND SAUCE
4 eating apples
90 g/3½ oz/scant ½ cup butter
225 g/8 oz/1⅓ cups light muscovado sugar
150 ml/¼ pint/⅔ cup double cream

1 Make the crêpe batter. Sift the flour and salt into a large bowl. Add the eggs and milk and beat until smooth. Stir in the cider and set the batter aside for 30 minutes.

2 Heat a small heavy-based non-stick frying pan. Add a knob of butter and ladle in enough batter to coat the pan thinly. Cook until the crêpe is golden underneath, then flip it over and cook the other side until golden. Slide the crêpe on to a plate. Repeat with the remaining mixture to make seven more crêpes. Keep warm.

3 Make the filling. Core the apples and cut them into thick slices. Heat 15 g/½ oz/1 tbsp of the butter in a large frying pan. Add the apples and cook until golden on both sides, then transfer the slices to a bowl with a slotted spoon and set them aside.

4 Add the rest of the butter to the pan. As soon as it has melted, add the muscovado sugar. When the sugar has dissolved and the mixture is bubbling, stir in the cream. Continue cooking until it forms a smooth sauce.

5 Fold each pancake in half, then fold in half again to form a cone. Fill each with some of the fried apples. Place two filled pancakes on each dessert plate, drizzle over some of the butterscotch sauce and serve at once.

VARIATION: You could just as easily use plums, pears, strawberries or bananas to fill the crêpes. If you like, add a touch of Grand Marnier to the apples towards the end of the cooking time.

Cherry Clafoutis

When fresh cherries are in season this makes a deliciously simple dessert for any occasion. Serve warm with a little yogurt or pouring cream.

Serves 6

INGREDIENTS
50 g/2 oz/¼ cup butter, melted
675 g/1½ lb fresh cherries
50 g/2 oz/½ cup plain flour
pinch of salt
4 eggs, plus 2 egg yolks
115 g/4 oz/½ cup caster sugar
600 ml/1 pint/2½ cups milk
caster sugar, for dusting (optional)
yogurt or pouring cream, to serve

1 Preheat the oven to 190°C/375°F/Gas 5. Lightly butter the base and sides of a shallow ovenproof dish. Stone the cherries and place in the dish.

VARIATION: Use two 425 g/15 oz cans stoned black cherries, thoroughly drained, if fresh cherries are not available. For a special dessert, add 45 ml/3 tbsp kirsch to the batter.

2 Sift the flour and salt into a large bowl. Add the eggs, egg yolks, caster sugar and a little of the milk and, using a balloon whisk, beat to a smooth batter ensuring that all the flour is incorporated.

3 Gradually whisk in the remaining milk and the rest of the butter, then strain the batter over the cherries.

4 Bake for 40–50 minutes, until the topping is golden and just set. Serve while still warm with yogurt or pouring cream, dusted with caster sugar, if you like.

Yellow Plum Tart

Glazed yellow plums sit atop a delectable almond filling in a crisp pastry shell. When they are in season, greengages make an excellent alternative to the plums and taste wonderful.

Serves 8

INGREDIENTS
175 g/6 oz/1½ cups plain flour, plus extra for dusting
pinch of salt
75 g/3 oz/6 tbsp butter, chilled
30 ml/2 tbsp caster sugar
a few drops of vanilla essence
45 ml/3 tbsp iced water
cream or custard, to serve

FOR THE FILLING
75 g/3 oz/⅓ cup caster sugar
75 g/3 oz/6 tbsp butter, softened
75 g/3 oz/¾ cup ground almonds
1 egg, beaten
30 ml/2 tbsp plain flour
450 g/1 lb yellow plums or greengages, halved and stoned

FOR THE GLAZE
45 ml/3 tbsp apricot jam, sieved
15 ml/1 tbsp water

1 Sift the flour and salt into a bowl, then rub in the butter until the mixture resembles fine breadcrumbs. Stir in the caster sugar, vanilla essence and enough of the iced water to make a soft dough.

2 Knead the dough gently on a lightly floured surface until smooth, then wrap in clear film and chill for 10 minutes.

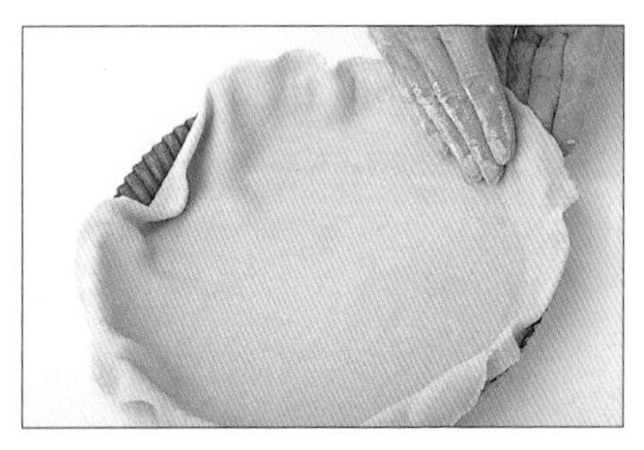

3 Preheat the oven to 200°C/400°F/Gas 6. Roll out the pastry and line a 23 cm/9 in fluted flan tin, allowing excess pastry to overhang the top. Prick the base with a fork and line with non-stick baking parchment and baking beans.

4 Bake blind for 10 minutes, remove the paper and beans, then return the pastry case to the oven for 10 minutes. Remove and allow to cool. Trim off any excess pastry with a sharp knife.

5 To make the filling, whisk together all the ingredients except the plums or greengages. Spread on the base of the pastry case. Arrange the fruit on top, placing it cut side down. Make a glaze by heating the jam with the water. Stir well, then brush a little of the jam glaze over the top of the fruit.

6 Bake the tart for 50–60 minutes, until the almond filling is cooked and the plums or greengages are tender. Warm any remaining jam glaze and brush it over the top. Cut into slices and serve with cream or custard.

Chocolate Chip & Banana Pudding

Hot and steamy, this superb light pudding has a beguiling banana and chocolate flavour that is sure to make it a family favourite.

Serves 4

INGREDIENTS
200 g/7 oz/1¾ cups self-raising flour
75 g/3 oz/6 tbsp unsalted butter or margarine
2 ripe bananas
75 g/3 oz/⅓ cup caster sugar
60 ml/4 tbsp milk
1 egg, beaten
60 ml/4 tbsp plain chocolate chips or chopped chocolate
chocolate sauce and whipped cream, to serve

1 Prepare a steamer or half fill a saucepan with water and bring it to the boil. Grease a 1 litre/1¾ pint/ 4 cup pudding basin. Sift the flour into a bowl and rub in the butter or margarine until the mixture resembles coarse breadcrumbs.

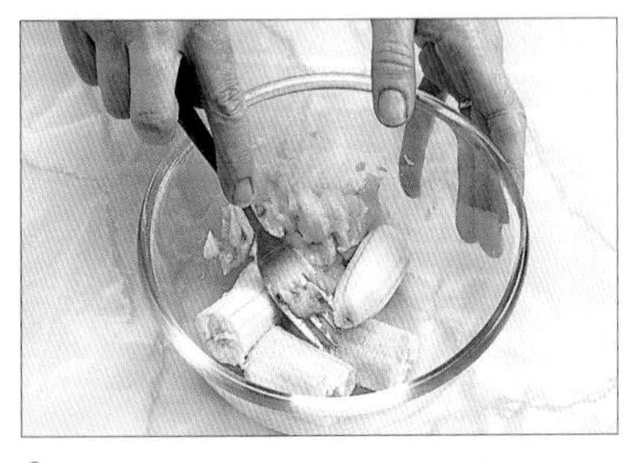

2 Mash the bananas in a bowl. Stir them into the flour and butter mixture, with the caster sugar.

3 Whisk the milk with the egg in a bowl, then beat into the pudding mixture. Stir in the chocolate.

4 Spoon into the prepared basin, cover closely with a double thickness of foil and steam for 2 hours, topping up the water as required.

5 Run a knife around the top of the pudding, turn out on to a dish and serve hot, with the sauce and cream.

COOK'S TIP: To make chocolate sauce, gently heat 115 g/4 oz/½ cup caster sugar with 60 ml/4 tbsp water in a saucepan, stirring occasionally, until the sugar has dissolved. Stir in 175 g/6 oz plain chocolate, a few squares at a time, until melted. Stir in 25 g/1 oz/2 tbsp butter, a little at a time, until melted. Stir in 30 ml/ 2 tbsp brandy or orange juice.

Lemon Surprise Pudding

This is a much-loved dessert many of us remember from childhood. The surprise is the unexpected sauce concealed beneath the delectable sponge.

Serves 4

INGREDIENTS
50 g/2 oz/¼ cup butter, plus extra for greasing
grated rind and juice of 2 lemons
115 g/4 oz/½ cup caster sugar
2 eggs, separated
50 g/2 oz/½ cup self-raising flour
300 ml/½ pint/1¼ cups milk

1 Preheat the oven to 190°C/375°F/Gas 5. Use a little butter to grease a 1.2 litre/2 pint/5 cup ovenproof dish.

2 Beat together the lemon rind, remaining butter and caster sugar in a bowl until pale and fluffy. Add the egg yolks and flour and beat together well. Gradually whisk in the lemon juice and milk.

3 In a greasefree bowl whisk the egg whites until they form stiff peaks. Fold the egg whites lightly into the lemon mixture, then pour into the prepared ovenproof dish.

4 Place the dish in a roasting tin and pour enough hot water into the tin to come halfway up the side of the dish. Bake the pudding for about 45 minutes, until golden. Serve at once.

COOK'S TIP: When whisking the lemon juice and milk into the pudding mixture, don't be alarmed if the mixture curdles. This is perfectly normal and will not affect the finished pudding.

Magic Chocolate Mud Pudding

A popular favourite, which magically separates into a light and luscious sponge and a velvety chocolate sauce.

Serves 4

INGREDIENTS
50 g/2 oz/¼ cup butter
200 g/7 oz/generous 1 cup light muscovado sugar
475 ml/16 fl oz/2 cups milk
90 g/3½ oz/scant 1 cup self-raising flour
5 ml/1 tsp ground cinnamon
75 ml/5 tbsp cocoa powder
Greek-style yogurt or vanilla ice cream, to serve

1 Preheat the oven to 180°C/350°F/Gas 4. Lightly grease a 1.5 litre/2½ pint/6¼ cup ovenproof dish and place on a baking sheet.

2 Place the butter in a saucepan. Add 115 g/4 oz/¾ cup of the sugar and 150 ml/¼ pint/⅔ cup of the milk. Heat gently, stirring occasionally, until the butter has melted and all the sugar has dissolved. Remove from the heat.

3 Sift the flour, ground cinnamon and 15 ml/1 tbsp of the cocoa into the pan and stir into the mixture, mixing evenly. Pour the mixture into the prepared dish and level the surface.

4 Sift the remaining sugar and cocoa powder into a bowl, mix well, then sprinkle over the pudding mixture in the dish. Pour the remaining milk over the pudding.

5 Bake for 45–50 minutes, or until the sponge has risen to the top and is firm to the touch. Serve the pudding hot, with the Greek-style yogurt or vanilla ice cream.

COOK'S TIP: A soufflé dish or similar straight-sided ovenproof dish is ideal for this pudding, since it supports the sponge as it rises above the sauce below.

Sticky Pear Pudding

Cloves add a distinctive fragrant flavour to this melt-in-the-mouth hazelnut, pear and coffee pudding.

Serves 6

INGREDIENTS
30 ml/2 tbsp ground coffee
15 ml/1 tbsp near-boiling water
50 g/2 oz/½ cup toasted skinned hazelnuts
4 ripe pears
juice of ½ orange
115 g/4 oz/½ cup butter, softened, plus extra, for greasing
115 g/4 oz/generous ½ cup golden caster sugar, plus an extra 15 ml/1 tbsp, for sprinkling
2 eggs, beaten
50 g/2 oz/½ cup self-raising flour, sifted
pinch of ground cloves
8 whole cloves
45 ml/3 tbsp maple syrup
fine strips of orange rind, to decorate

FOR THE ORANGE CREAM
300 ml/½ pint/1¼ cups whipping cream
15 ml/1 tbsp icing sugar, sifted
finely grated rind of ½ orange

1 Preheat the oven to 180°C/350°F/ Gas 4. Lightly grease a 20 cm/8 in loose-based sandwich tin. Put the coffee in a small bowl with the water. Infuse for 4 minutes, then strain.

2 Finely grind the hazelnuts. Peel, halve and core the pears. Thinly slice across the pear halves part of the way through. Brush with orange juice.

3 Beat the softened butter and the 115 g/4 oz/generous ½ cup caster sugar together in a bowl until light and fluffy. Gradually beat in the eggs, then fold in the flour, ground cloves, hazelnuts and coffee. Spoon the mixture into the tin and level the surface.

4 Pat the pears dry on kitchen paper, and press one clove into the hollow of each pear, then arrange in the sponge mixture, flat side down. Brush the pears with 15 ml/1 tbsp maple syrup.

5 Sprinkle the pears with the 15 ml/ 1 tbsp caster sugar. Bake the pudding for 45–50 minutes, until firm and risen.

6 Meanwhile, make the orange cream. Whip the cream, icing sugar and orange rind until soft peaks form. Spoon into a serving dish and chill until needed.

7 Allow the sponge to cool for about 10 minutes in the tin, then remove and place on a serving plate. Brush with the remaining maple syrup before serving warm with the orange cream and decorating with orange rind.

Steamed Ginger & Cinnamon Syrup Pudding

A traditional and comforting steamed pudding, best served with custard on a chilly winter's evening.

Serves 4

INGREDIENTS
120 g/4¼ oz/9 tbsp softened butter
45 ml/3 tbsp golden syrup
115 g/4 oz/½ cup
caster sugar
2 eggs, lightly beaten
115 g/4 oz/1 cup plain flour
5 ml/1 tsp baking powder
5 ml/1 tsp ground cinnamon
25 g/1 oz stem ginger,
finely chopped
30 ml/2 tbsp milk

1 Set a full steamer or saucepan of water on to boil. Lightly grease a 600 ml/1 pint/2½ cup pudding basin with 15 g/½ oz/1 tbsp butter. Pour the golden syrup into the basin.

2 Cream the remaining butter and sugar until light and fluffy. Gradually beat in the eggs until the mixture is glossy. Sift the dry ingredients together and fold into the mixture with the ginger. Add the milk to make a dropping consistency.

3 Spoon the batter into the basin and smooth the top. Cover with a pleated piece of greaseproof paper to allow for expansion. Tie with string and steam for 1½–2 hours, topping up the water level. Turn out to serve.

This edition published by Southwater

Distributed in the UK by
The Manning Partnership, 251-253 London Road East, Batheaston, Bath BA1 7RL, UK
tel. (0044) 01225 852 727 fax. (0044) 01225 852 852

Distributed in the USA by
Ottenheimer Publishing, 5 Park Center Court, Suite 300, Owing Mills MD 2117-5001, USA
tel. (001) 410 902 9100 fax. (001) 410 902 7210

Distributed in Australia by
Sandstone Publishing, Unit 1, 360 Norton Street, Leichhardt, New South Wales 2040, Australia
tel. (0061) 2 9560 7888 fax. (0061) 2 9560 7488

Distributed in New Zealand by
Five Mile Press NZ, PO Box 33-1071, Takapuna, Auckland 9, New Zealand
tel. (0064) 9 4444 144 fax. (0064) 4444 518

Southwater is an imprint of Anness Publishing Limited

A CIP catalogue record for this book is available from the British Library.

Publisher: Joanna Lorenz
Editor: Valerie Ferguson
Series Designer: Bobbie Colgate Stone
Designer: Andrew Heath
Editorial Reader: Joy Wotton
Production Controller: Joanna King

Recipes Contributed by: Catherine Atkinson, Janet Brinkworth, Kathy Brown, Carol Clements, Joanna Farrow, Christine France, Sarah Gates, Lesley Mackley, Maggie Mayhew, Liz Trigg, Steven Wheeler, Elizabeth Wolf-Cohen.

Photography: Karl Adamson, Edward Allwright, Steve Baxter, Louise Dare, Michelle Garrett, Amanda Heywood, Don Last, William Lingwood, Polly Wreford.

1 3 5 7 9 10 8 6 4 2

Notes:
For all recipes, quantities are given in both metric and imperial measures and, where appropriate, measures are also given in standard cups and spoons.
Follow one set, but not a mixture, because they are not interchangeable.

Standard spoon and cup measures are level.
1 tsp = 5 ml 1 tbsp = 15 ml
1 cup = 250 ml/8 fl oz
Australian standard tablespoons are 20 ml.
Australian readers should use 3 tsp in place of 1 tbsp for measuring small quantities of gelatine, cornflour, salt, etc.
Medium eggs are used unless otherwise stated.

Printed and bound in Singapore